Our Favorite
30-Minute Meals

Copyright 2013, Gooseberry Patch
First Printing, December, 2013

No-mess stuffed shells! Instead of a spoon, use a pastry bag
to fill cooked pasta shells...they'll be ready in no time.

Renae's Cheesy Shells

Serves 4 to 6

1 lb. ground beef, browned
   and drained
1 c. instant rice, cooked
1 c. spaghetti sauce
1 c. cottage cheese
1 t. garlic powder

1/4 t. salt
1 c. shredded Cheddar cheese,
   divided
12-oz. pkg. jumbo pasta shells,
   cooked

Combine all ingredients except shredded cheese and pasta shells in a
large bowl. Add 1/2 cup shredded cheese and mix well. Spoon mixture
into cooked shells. Arrange shells in a lightly greased 13"x9" baking pan;
sprinkle with remaining shredded cheese. Bake, covered, at 350 degrees
for 25 to 30 minutes.

A quick, refreshing cooler to go with Gingered Broccoli Beef...
steep 8 mint teabags in 2 cups of boiling water. Add 2 cups of
orange juice, 1-1/2 cups lemonade, 2 cups crushed ice and
2 cans of ginger ale. Garnish with orange slices.

Gingered Broccoli Beef

Makes 4 servings

1 bunch broccoli, cut into
　　flowerets
1 lb. beef tenderloin, sliced into
　　thin strips
1 T. fresh ginger, peeled and
　　grated
3 cloves garlic, pressed

1/4 t. red pepper flakes
1 to 2 t. olive oil
3/4 c. chicken broth
3 T. soy sauce
1 T. cornstarch
1/2 t. sesame oil

Cover broccoli with water in a saucepan. Bring to a boil and cook until crisp-tender, about 3 to 5 minutes. Drain; set aside and cover to keep warm. Toss beef with ginger, garlic and red pepper flakes. Add oil to a skillet over medium-high heat. Add beef mixture and cook for 2 to 3 minutes, stirring constantly, until beef is lightly browned. Whisk together remaining ingredients and add to skillet; heat to boiling. Cook and stir for one minute, or until sauce thickens slightly. Add broccoli and toss to coat.

Love cabbage...but don't love the aroma? Use an old-fashioned trick to keep your house sweet-smelling. Just add a spoonful of vinegar, a lemon wedge or half an apple to the cooking pot.

Russian Hot Pot

Serves 6

2 c. water
2 cubes beef bouillon
1 lb. redskin potatoes, cut into
    1/2-inch cubes
1 lb. cabbage, cut into
    1/2-inch cubes

1 onion, quartered
16-oz. can whole tomatoes,
    drained
1-1/2 lbs. lean ground beef

Combine water and bouillon in a Dutch oven; bring to a boil over medium-high heat. Add potatoes and increase heat to high. Add cabbage, onion and tomatoes, breaking up tomatoes with your fingers. Add uncooked beef, crumbling it up. Boil for about 30 seconds; stir to mix well. Cover; reduce heat and simmer about 30 minutes, or until potatoes are tender. To serve, ladle into soup bowls.

Vintage milk bottles make clever last-minute vases. Fill with
small bouquets of cut flowers from the garden and
line up a few down the center of the table.

Beef & Cheese Foldover

Serves 4 to 6

1 lb. ground beef
1 onion, chopped
1 c. corn
16-oz. can black beans,
    drained and rinsed
1/4 c. catsup

2 T. steak sauce
2 c. biscuit baking mix
1/2 c. hot water
1 c. shredded Mexican-blend
    cheese
Optional: 1/2 t. dried parsley

In a skillet over medium heat, brown beef with onion; drain. Stir in corn, beans, catsup and steak sauce; set aside. In a bowl, stir baking mix and water together until dough forms. Form into a ball. Place on a lightly floured surface; knead 5 times, or until smooth and no longer sticky. Roll into a 12-inch circle; transfer to a lightly greased baking sheet. Spoon beef mixture onto center of dough; spread to within 2 inches of the edge. Fold edge of dough over beef mixture, leaving center uncovered. Bake, uncovered, at 375 degrees for 20 minutes. Remove from oven; sprinkle with cheese. Bake an additional 5 minutes, or until cheese is melted. Sprinkle with parsley, if using.

For a simple, sweetly scented place setting, tie a few cinnamon sticks together with raffia, attach a mailing label as a name card and lay a bundle across each plate.

Filet Mignon with Mushrooms

Makes 4 servings

4 6-oz. beef filet mignon steaks	12-oz. pkg. sliced mushrooms
1/2 t. salt	4 cloves garlic, chopped
1/2 t. pepper	1/4 c. plus 2 T. Marsala wine or
1/2 t. garlic powder	beef broth

Sprinkle each steak with salt, pepper and garlic powder; set aside. Coat a large skillet with non-stick vegetable spray and heat to medium-high. Add mushrooms and garlic; cook, stirring frequently for 5 minutes or until mushrooms are golden. Remove from heat and set aside. Arrange steaks on a broiler pan about 4 inches below the heat source. Broil for about 4 minutes on each side, or to desired doneness. In skillet, reheat mushroom mixture over medium-high heat. Add wine or broth to mixture and bring to a boil; cook for about 2 minutes, until liquid is reduced. Place each steak on a serving plate and top with mushroom mixture.

When the zucchini harvest is at its peak, freeze extras
for use all winter long. Shred zucchini, then steam it for one to
2 minutes. Cool and pack pre-measured amounts into containers,
leaving 1/2-inch headspace. Seal, label and freeze. When using
in a recipe, thaw and add to ingredients, reducing the
amount of liquid if needed.

Zucchini & Beef in Wine Sauce

Serves 4

2 to 3 T. olive oil, divided
1 lb. stew beef cubes
2 cloves garlic, minced
1 onion, sliced
1 zucchini, halved lengthwise
    and sliced into crescents

1/2 yellow pepper, chopped
1 red pepper, chopped
salt and pepper to taste
2-1/2 t. red wine or beef broth
Optional: grated Parmesan cheese

Heat 2 tablespoons oil in a skillet over medium heat; brown beef in oil. Add garlic and sauté. Stir in onion, zucchini and peppers; mix well and add salt and pepper to taste. Cook for about 15 to 20 minutes, adding more oil as needed. Stir in wine or broth. If desired, sprinkle with Parmesan cheese before serving.

Out of biscuit baking mix? No problem! For each cup needed in a recipe, use 1 cup all-purpose flour, 1-1/2 teaspoons baking powder, 1/2 teaspoon salt and 1 tablespoon shortening.

Sloppy Joe Bake

Serves 8

1-1/2 lbs. ground beef
1/4 c. onion, chopped
1/4 c. green pepper, chopped
15-1/2 oz. can Sloppy Joe sauce
8-oz. pkg. shredded Cheddar
    cheese

2 c. biscuit baking mix
2 eggs, beaten
1 c. milk

In a skillet over medium heat, brown beef, onion and green pepper; drain. Stir in sauce. Spoon mixture into a greased 13"x9" baking pan; sprinkle with cheese. In a bowl, stir together remaining ingredients just until blended. Spoon over cheese. Bake, uncovered, at 400 degrees for about 25 minutes, until golden. Cut into squares.

Flour tortillas are tastiest when warmed. Stack tortillas
between moistened paper towels and microwave on
high setting for 20 to 30 seconds...easy!

Simple & Hearty Burritos

Serves 6 to 8

1 lb. ground beef or Italian
    ground pork sausage
15-oz. can chili
16-oz. can refried beans
2 to 4 T. taco seasoning mix

8 10-inch flour tortillas
Garnish: shredded cheese,
    chopped tomato, chopped
    onion, shredded lettuce,
    sour cream, salsa

Brown beef or sausage in a skillet over medium heat; drain. Add chili, beans and desired amount of taco seasoning to skillet. Mix well. Cook until hot and bubbly. Fill tortillas with mixture; add any desired toppings and roll into burritos.

Keep browned ground beef on hand for easy meal prep.
Just crumble several pounds of beef into a baking pan and
bake at 350 degrees until browned through, stirring often.
Drain well and pack recipe-size portions in freezer bags.

Chris's Vegetable Beef Soup

Makes about 8 servings

1 lb. ground beef
1 onion, chopped
2 to 4 stalks celery, chopped
3 T. olive oil
15-oz. can diced tomatoes
14-1/2 oz. can diced potatoes,
    drained
1 clove garlic, pressed
14-oz. pkg. frozen mixed
    vegetables
5 c. beef broth
Optional: 1 c. bowtie pasta,
    uncooked

Place beef, onion, celery and oil in a Dutch oven; brown well over medium heat. Drain; add remaining ingredients. Simmer over medium heat until vegetables are tender, about 10 minutes.

Try using a different shape of pasta next time you make Chili Mac Skillet. Wagon wheels, seashells and bow ties all hold cheese sauce well...they're fun for kids too!

Chili Mac Skillet

Makes 4 to 6 servings

1 onion, chopped
1 to 2 t. oil
1 lb. ground beef
seasoning salt to taste
1/2 c. elbow macaroni, uncooked
15-oz. can kidney beans, drained
    and rinsed

8-oz. can tomato sauce
4-oz. can diced green chiles
1/4 c. water
1 T. chili powder
1/2 t. garlic powder
1 c. shredded Cheddar cheese

In a skillet over medium heat, sauté onion in oil. Add beef and seasoning salt. Cook until beef is browned; drain. Stir in remaining ingredients except cheese. Bring to a boil; reduce heat. Cover and simmer for 20 minutes, stirring often, until macaroni is tender. Remove from heat; sprinkle with cheese, cover and let stand until cheese is melted, about 2 minutes.

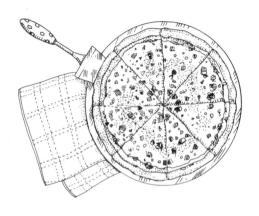

Make assembly part of pizza night fun! Prepare the crust,
then set out the sauce, pepperoni, veggies, seasonings and
cheese. Let family members add toppings as they like
even little ones can help out. Bake, slice and dinner's ready!

Deep-Dish Pizza

Serves 6 to 8

1 lb. ground beef
1/2 c. onion, chopped
2 cloves garlic, minced
2 8-1/2 oz. pkgs. pizza crust mix
14-oz. jar pizza sauce
4-oz. can sliced mushrooms,
    drained

1/4 c. green pepper, chopped
3.8-oz. can sliced black olives,
    drained
2-1/2 c. shredded mozzarella
    cheese

In a skillet over medium heat, brown beef with onion and garlic until beef is no longer pink. Drain; set aside. Prepare pizza crust according to package directions. Transfer dough to a greased 13"x9" baking pan, pressing halfway up sides of the pan. Pierce dough several times with a fork. Bake at 425 degrees for 5 minutes; remove from oven. Cover with sauce; layer with beef mixture, mushrooms, green pepper, olives and cheese. Bake, uncovered, at 425 degrees for 20 to 25 minutes, until cheese is melted.

To mix up a no-mess meatloaf, place all the ingredients in
a large plastic zipping bag. Seal the bag and squish it until
everything is well combined...then just toss the empty bag!

Easy Mini Meatloaves

Makes 10 servings.

12-oz. tube refrigerated biscuits
1-1/2 lbs. ground beef
1 c. catsup, divided
1/2 c. onion, chopped

1 egg, beaten
1/4 c. quick-cooking oats,
   uncooked
1 c. shredded Cheddar cheese

Divide and press biscuit dough into the bottom and up the sides of
10 greased muffin cups; set aside. In a bowl, combine beef, 1/2 cup
catsup, onion, egg and oats; mix well. Form beef mixture into 10 balls;
place one in each muffin cup. Spread remaining catsup over top; sprinkle
with cheese. Bake, uncovered, at 350 degrees for 30 minutes, or until
no longer pink in the center.

Everybody loves burgers...and they don't have to be ordinary!
Ground turkey, chicken, ground pork sausage and veggie
burgers are all scrumptious. Try the seasoning blends
found at the meat counter like Italian, Mexican, Southwest
or Mediterranean...yum!

Key West Burgers

1 lb. ground beef
3 T. Key lime juice
1/4 c. fresh cilantro, chopped

salt and pepper to taste
hamburger buns, split and toasted
Garnish: lettuce

In a bowl, combine beef, lime juice, cilantro, salt and pepper. Form into 4 patties. Spray a skillet with non-stick vegetable spray. Cook patties over medium heat for 6 minutes. Flip patties, cover skillet and cook for another 6 minutes. Place lettuce on bottom halves of buns and top with patties. Add Creamy Burger Spread; close sandwiches.

Creamy Burger Spread:

8-oz. pkg. cream cheese, softened
8-oz. container sour cream

3 green onion tops, chopped

Combine all ingredients until completely blended. Cover and refrigerate at least 15 minutes.

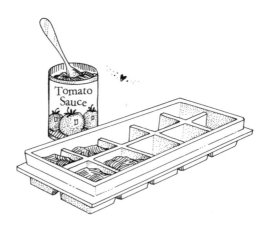

To keep pasta sauce (Alfredo or tomato) on hand
in small amounts, freeze it in ice cube trays. Once frozen,
transfer cubes to a freezer bag. Two cubes are
the perfect amount for one cup of pasta.

Big Eddie's Rigatoni

Serves 8

16-oz. pkg. rigatoni pasta,
    uncooked
1/8 t. salt
2 lbs. lean ground beef
1-1/2 oz. pkg. spaghetti sauce
    mix
45-oz. jar chunky tomato, garlic
    and onion pasta sauce

8 slices mozzarella cheese,
    divided
8 slices provolone cheese, divided
8-oz. container sour cream
Garnish: grated Parmesan cheese

Cook pasta according to package directions; drain, mix in salt and set aside. Meanwhile, in a large, deep skillet over medium heat, brown beef; drain. Stir in spaghetti sauce mix and pasta sauce; heat through. In a greased 13"x9" baking pan, layer half the pasta, 4 slices mozzarella cheese and 4 slices provolone cheese. Spread entire container of sour cream across top. Layer half of beef mixture. Repeat layering, except for sour cream, ending with beef mixture. Garnish with Parmesan cheese. Bake, uncovered, at 350 degrees for 30 minutes, or until bubbly.

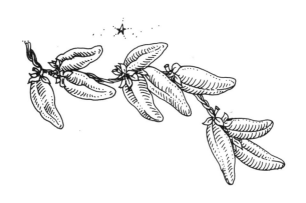

Visit a local Mexican grocery or stroll the Mexican food aisle
in your favorite grocery store! You'll be inspired.

Mexican Shepherd's Pie

Makes 6 servings

7-oz. pkg. 4-cheese instant
    mashed potato flakes
1 lb. lean ground beef
1/2 c. green onions, sliced and
    divided
1 c. barbecue sauce
4-oz. can chopped green chiles

11-oz. can sweet corn & diced
    peppers, drained and divided
1-1/2 c. hot water
1/3 c. milk
2 T. butter
1/2 c. shredded Cheddar cheese
1 c. corn chips

Set aside one pouch of instant mashed potato flakes for future use. Cook beef and half the onions in a skillet over medium-high heat, stirring occasionally, until beef is browned; drain. Stir in barbecue sauce, chiles and 3/4 cup corn & diced peppers. Heat to boiling; reduce heat to low. Meanwhile, prepare one pouch instant mashed potato flakes according to package directions, using hot water, milk and butter. Stir in remaining onions and corn & diced peppers; let stand 5 minutes. Spoon potatoes over beef mixture; sprinkle with cheese. Cover, remove from heat and let stand 5 minutes, or until cheese is melted. Sprinkle with corn chips.

Make your own taco seasoning mix! In a jar, combine
3/4 cup dried, minced onion, 1/4 cup each salt and chili powder,
2 tablespoons each cornstarch, red pepper flakes, ground cumin
and dried, minced garlic and one tablespoon dried oregano.
Four tablespoons of mix equals a 1-1/4 ounce envelope.

Taco Pasta Skillet

Serves 6

1/2 lb. lean ground beef, browned
   and drained
1-1/4 oz. pkg. taco seasoning mix
11-oz. can corn, drained
14-oz. can black beans, drained
   and rinsed

1 c. salsa
3 c. hot water
1 c. penne pasta, uncooked
1/2 c. cream cheese, softened
1 c. shredded Mexican-blend
   cheese

Place all ingredients except cheeses in a large, deep skillet over medium heat; mix well. Simmer for 15 minutes, or until pasta is tender. Stir in cheeses and continue to cook until cheese is melted.

Dress up a tube of refrigerated bread stick dough. Before baking, brush the dough with a little beaten egg, then sprinkle with sesame seeds, grated Parmesan or dried rosemary. A great accompaniment to soup or pasta!

Deb's Chicken Florentine

Makes 6 servings

16-oz. pkg. linguine pasta,
    uncooked
2 T. olive oil
3 cloves garlic, minced
4 boneless, skinless chicken
    breasts, thinly sliced
1-1/4 c. fat-free zesty Italian
    salad dressing, divided

8 sun-dried tomatoes, chopped
8-oz. pkg. sliced mushrooms
5-oz. pkg. baby spinach
cracked pepper to taste
Optional: grated Parmesan
    cheese, chopped fresh
    flat-leaf parsley

Cook pasta according to package directions; drain. While pasta is cooking, warm oil in a skillet over medium heat. Add garlic and cook 2 minutes. Add chicken; cook until no longer pink. Drizzle chicken with one cup salad dressing. Stir in tomatoes and mushrooms; cover skillet and simmer until mushrooms are softened. Add spinach; cover and cook another 2 to 3 minutes, just until spinach is wilted; stir and sprinkle with pepper. Toss cooked linguine with remaining salad dressing. Serve chicken and vegetables over linguine, garnished as desired.

For the quickest-ever candlelit atmosphere, set several lighted
tea lights on the table and top them with metal cheese graters.
They'll cast the same twinkling glow as pierced tin lanterns.

Skillet Chicken Cordon Bleu

Serves 4 to 6

2 T. margarine
4 to 6 boneless, skinless chicken
    breasts
salt and pepper to taste
.87-oz. pkg. chicken gravy mix

3/4 c. water
1/4 c. dry white wine or
    apple juice
1/4 c. deli ham, chopped
1/4 c. shredded Swiss cheese

In a skillet over medium heat, melt margarine. Season chicken with salt and pepper and cook in margarine for 5 minutes, or until browned; drain. In a bowl, combine gravy mix, water, wine or juice and ham. Pour gravy mixture over chicken in skillet. Reduce heat and simmer, partially covered, for 15 to 20 minutes, until chicken is cooked through. Remove chicken to a broiler pan; sprinkle with cheese and broil until cheese is melted. Serve chicken with gravy mixture.

Mix up your own Italian seasoning for pasta dishes, soups, salads and garlic bread. A good basic blend is 2 tablespoons each of dried oregano, thyme, basil, marjoram and rosemary...add or subtract to suit your family's taste. Store in a big shaker jar.

Chicken & Rosemary Pizza

Serves 4 to 6

2 c. shredded mozzarella cheese, divided
2 c. cooked chicken, chopped
1 c. red onion, sliced
1/4 c. fresh parsley, chopped
2 T. olive oil

2 cloves garlic, minced
1 T. fresh rosemary, chopped
1/2 t. salt
1/4 t. pepper
13.8-oz. tube refrigerated pizza dough

In a bowl, toss together 1-1/2 cups cheese and remaining ingredients except pizza dough; set aside. Roll out dough onto a lightly greased baking sheet. Spread cheese mixture onto dough to within 1/2 inch of the edge. Sprinkle with remaining cheese. Bake at 425 degrees for 18 to 22 minutes, until golden. Let stand 10 minutes before slicing.

White paper coffee filters make tidy toss-away holders
for hot dog buns, sandwiches or tacos.

Turkey & Berry Sandwiches

Serves 2

2 lettuce leaves
2 slices Swiss cheese
1/4 lb. thinly sliced deli turkey
4 strawberries, hulled and sliced

4 slices whole-wheat bread
2 T. whipped cream cheese spread
2 t. pecans, finely chopped

Layer lettuce, cheese, turkey and strawberries on 2 slices of bread.
Combine cream cheese and pecans. Spread over remaining bread slices;
close sandwiches.

Dill is a delicate yet savory flavor that's perfect in potato
and chicken soups, egg and potato salads, and sprinkled on
cucumbers and steamed carrots. It's also wonderful in breads.

Dilly Chicken Sandwiches

Makes 4 servings

4 boneless, skinless chicken
    breasts
6 T. butter, softened and divided
1 clove garlic, minced
3/4 t. dill weed, divided

8 slices French bread
1/4 c. cream cheese, softened
2 t. lemon juice
Garnish: lettuce leaves, tomato
    slices, bread & butter pickles

Place one chicken breast between 2 pieces of wax paper. Using a mallet, flatten to 1/4-inch thickness. Repeat with remaining chicken; set aside. In a skillet over medium-high heat, melt 3 tablespoons butter; stir in garlic and 1/2 teaspoon dill weed. Add chicken; cook on both sides until juices run clear. Remove and keep warm. Spread both sides of bread with remaining butter. On a griddle, grill bread on both sides until golden. Combine remaining ingredients except garnish; spread on one side of 4 slices grilled bread. Top with chicken; garnish as desired. Top with remaining bread.

Honey comes in lots of flavor varieties. Seek out a local beekeeper at the farmers' market and try a few samples... you may find a new favorite!

Honey Chicken Stir-Fry

Serves 4 to 6

1 to 2 lbs. boneless, skinless
    chicken strips
4 T. honey, divided
1 egg, beaten
1/3 c. plus 1 T. water, divided
1 t. Worcestershire sauce
1/2 t. dried thyme
1/4 t. lemon-pepper seasoning
1/4 t. garlic powder

1/8 t. dried oregano
1/8 t. dried marjoram
2 T. oil
1 T. cornstarch
16-oz. pkg. frozen stir-fry
    vegetables
1/4 t. salt
cooked rice

Combine chicken, 2 tablespoons honey, egg, 1/3 cup water, sauce and
seasonings; set aside. Heat oil in a wok or large skillet over medium-high
heat. Add chicken a few pieces at a time; cook and stir until golden.
Remove chicken from wok; keep warm. Mix cornstarch with remaining
honey and water; set aside. Add vegetables to wok; sprinkle with salt.
Cook over medium heat until vegetables begin to thaw; drizzle with
cornstarch mixture. Continue cooking until vegetables are tender; stir in
chicken and heat through. Serve with rice.

Carrot curls make a colorful garnish for soups! Cut long, thin
strips with a vegetable peeler, roll up and secure with
a toothpick. Soak in ice water for two hours...so easy!

Chicken Noodle Bowl

Makes 4 servings

8-oz. pkg. linguine pasta, uncooked
3 c. frozen broccoli cuts
2 carrots, peeled and sliced
2 t. oil

1 lb. boneless, skinless chicken breasts, cut into strips
1/2 c. zesty Italian salad dressing
1/3 c. teriyaki sauce
1 t. ground ginger

Cook pasta as package directs; add broccoli and carrots to the cooking water for last 2 minutes of cooking time. Drain pasta mixture. Meanwhile, heat oil in a large skillet over medium heat. Add chicken; cook, stirring occasionally, until golden on all sides and no longer pink in the center. Stir in remaining ingredients; cook until sauce thickens, stirring occasionally. Add pasta mixture to skillet. Stir until coated with sauce. Serve in individual bowls.

For a quick & tasty side, slice fresh tomatoes in half and sprinkle with minced garlic, Italian seasoning and grated Parmesan cheese. Broil until tomatoes are tender, about 5 minutes...scrumptious!

Stuffed Chicken Breasts

Serves 4

4 boneless, skinless chicken
    breasts
8-oz. container garlic & herb
    cream cheese spread

8 slices bacon

Flatten chicken breasts between wax paper. Spread each chicken breast with cream cheese and roll up. Wrap 2 slices bacon around each roll; secure with toothpicks. Place on a grill or in a grill pan over medium heat. Cook, turning occasionally, until golden and chicken juices run clear, about 20 to 25 minutes.

Pick up prepared stuffing in the meat section at your grocer.
It's ready to bake...you just top chicken breasts or
spoon alongside a turkey breast!

Thanksgiving in a Pan

6-oz. pkg stuffing mix
2-1/2 c. cooked turkey, cubed
2 c. frozen green beans, thawed

12-oz. jar turkey gravy
pepper to taste

Prepare stuffing mix according to package directions. Transfer to a greased 11"x7" baking pan. Layer with remaining ingredients in order listed. Cover and bake at 350 degrees for 30 to 35 minutes, until heated through.

A roast chicken from the deli is the busy cook's secret
ingredient! The chicken is already cooked and ready
for whatever recipe you decide to make.

Almost-Homemade Chicken & Noodles

Serves 8

7 c. chicken broth, divided
3/4 t. salt
1/2 t. pepper
24-oz. pkg. frozen homestyle egg
    noodles, uncooked

2 T. all-purpose flour
1 deli roast chicken, boned
    and chopped

In a large pot, combine 6 cups broth, salt and pepper. Bring to a boil over high heat. Add noodles; boil, uncovered, for 15 minutes, stirring occasionally. In a bowl, whisk together remaining broth and flour until smooth. Stir into broth mixture. Cook until thickened and bubbly, stirring occasionally. Add chicken. Cook 5 minutes more, or until heated through, stirring occasionally.

A speedy side for any south-of-the-border supper! Stir spicy salsa and shredded Mexican-blend cheese into hot cooked rice. Cover and let stand a few minutes until the cheese melts.

Soft Chicken Tacos

Makes 8 to 10

1 deli roast chicken, boned and
    shredded
15-oz. can black beans, drained
    and rinsed
1-1/2 T. taco seasoning mix

1 to 1-1/2 c. salsa
8 to 10 8-inch flour tortillas
Garnishes: shredded Cheddar
    cheese, sour cream,
    guacamole

Combine chicken, beans, taco seasoning and salsa; cook in a skillet
over medium heat until bubbly. Fill tortillas with chicken mixture;
garnish as desired.

Ahhh, soup & bread! Stop by the bakery for a fresh loaf of bread. Warmed slightly in the oven and topped with real butter, it's heavenly with any dinner!

Savory Chicken Stew

Makes 4 to 6 servings

1 onion, chopped
1 green pepper, chopped
1 T. oil
1/2 c. all-purpose flour
1/4 t. onion powder
1/4 t. paprika

1/4 t. salt
1/4 t. pepper
2 lbs. boneless, skinless chicken, cubed
8-oz. can tomato sauce
1/2 c. chicken broth

In a large skillet over medium heat, sauté onion and green pepper in oil until soft, about 5 minutes. Remove onion and pepper from skillet; set aside. Mix flour and seasonings in a large plastic zipping bag. Add chicken cubes; close bag and shake to coat chicken. Transfer chicken to skillet; cook until golden on both sides. Return onion and pepper to skillet; stir in sauce and broth. Cover and simmer for 10 to 15 minutes, until chicken is done.

Just for fun, serve up soft pretzels instead of dinner rolls. Twist strips of refrigerated bread stick dough into pretzel shapes and place on an ungreased baking sheet. Brush with beaten egg white, sprinkle with coarse salt and bake as directed.

Hillary's Pretzel Chicken

Makes 4 to 6 servings

1-1/2 c. pretzels
1/4 c. butter, melted
4 to 6 boneless, skinless chicken
  breasts

Garnish: honey mustard or other
  favorite mustard

Place pretzels in a plastic zipping bag; seal. With a mallet, crush finely.
Place melted butter in a shallow bowl. Dip chicken into butter; add to
crushed pretzels in zipping bag and coat well. Place chicken in a greased
13"x9" baking pan. Bake, uncovered, at 350 degrees for about 20 to
25 minutes, until chicken juices run clear. Serve with mustard for dipping.

An old cast-iron skillet is wonderful for cooking up homestyle
dinners. If it hasn't been used in awhile, season it first. Rub it
lightly with oil, bake at 300 degrees for an hour and let it
cool completely in the oven. Now it's ready for many more
years of good cooking!

Chicken Fajita Fettuccine

Serves 4

8-oz. pkg. fettuccine pasta,
    uncooked
1 T. olive oil
1 lb. boneless, skinless chicken
    breasts, cut into strips
1/2 c. mesquite-flavored marinade

16-oz. pkg. frozen stir-fry
    vegetables with peppers and
    onions
2 c. shredded Colby Jack cheese
Garnish: salsa, sour cream,
    guacamole

Cook pasta according to package directions; drain and set aside.
Heat oil over medium-high heat in a large skillet. Add chicken; cook
for 5 minutes. Stir in marinade and vegetables; sauté 10 minutes, or
until chicken is no longer pink in the center. In a large serving bowl,
toss chicken mixture with pasta and cheese. Serve immediately,
garnished as desired.

Make your own tortilla chips to go with homemade salsas
and dips...you won't believe how easy it is. Just slice flour tortillas
into wedges, spray with non-stick vegetable spray and bake at
350 degrees for 5 to 7 minutes.

Chicken Chilaquiles

Makes 6 to 8 servings

1/2 c. oil
10 corn tortillas, cut into 1/2-inch
    strips
Optional: salt to taste
1 c. shredded mozzarella cheese

1 c. shredded Cheddar cheese
2 c. cooked chicken, shredded
28-oz. can mild chile verde sauce,
    divided

Heat oil in a skillet over medium heat. Cook tortilla strips in oil, a few at a time, just until crispy. Drain tortilla strips on paper towels; sprinkle with salt, if desired. Mix cheeses in a bowl; set aside. Spray a 13"x9" baking pan with non-stick vegetable spray. Layer half of the tortilla strips in pan; top with chicken, one cup sauce and one cup cheese mixture. Press layers gently down into pan. Repeat layering with remaining tortilla strips, sauce and cheese. Bake, uncovered, at 350 degrees for about 30 minutes, until cheese is melted and golden.

The sweet, peppery flavor of basil goes with almost any dish, so keep some potted basil on your windowsill to snip any time of year!

Basil Chicken Skillet

Serves 4

2 boneless, skinless chicken
    breasts, diced
2 t. garlic, minced
1 onion, chopped
1 to 2 T. oil
14-oz. can diced tomatoes

2 c. chicken broth
1 t. dried basil, crushed
1/4 t. pepper
8-oz. pkg. spaghetti, uncooked
    and broken in half
1/4 c. grated Parmesan cheese

In a large skillet over medium heat, cook chicken, garlic and onion in oil until chicken is golden and onion is tender. Add tomatoes with juice, broth, basil and pepper to skillet. Bring to a boil. Stir in spaghetti, making sure spaghetti is covered by liquid. Reduce heat; cover and simmer for 15 to 20 minutes, until spaghetti is tender and chicken is no longer pink. Sprinkle with Parmesan cheese before serving.

Jams and preserves keep well, so pick up a few jars of local specialties like beach plum, peach or boysenberry on family vacations. Later, use them to bake up jam bars, linzer cookies or thumbprints...the flavors will bring back happy family memories!

Honeyed Raspberry Pork Chops

Serves 4

4 boneless pork chops
2 T. all-purpose flour
1/3 c. honey mustard
1/4 c. raspberry jam

2 T. cider vinegar
1 T. olive oil
1 T. fresh parsley, chopped

Dredge pork chops in flour, shaking off any excess. In a small bowl, combine mustard, jam and vinegar; set aside. Heat oil in a large skillet over medium heat. Add pork chops and sauté until golden on both sides. Stir in mustard mixture; bring to a boil. Reduce heat and simmer for 10 minutes, until pork chops are no longer pink in the center. Sprinkle with parsley.

Quick & easy appetizers...wrap pear slices with prosciutto or
melon wedges with thinly-sliced turkey. Ready in a snap!

Scott's Ham & Pear Sandwiches *Makes 4 sandwiches*

8 slices sourdough bread
4 slices Swiss cheese
1-1/4 lbs. sliced deli ham

15-oz. can pear halves, drained
and thinly sliced

Spread each bread slice with a thin layer of Spiced Butter. On each of 4 slices, place one slice of cheese; layer evenly with ham and pears. Top with remaining bread slices and press together gently. Spread the outside of the sandwiches with desired amount of Spiced Butter. Heat a large skillet over medium-high heat and cook until crisp and golden, about 5 minutes on each side.

Spiced Butter:

1 c. butter, softened
2 t. pumpkin pie spice
1 t. ground coriander

1 t. ground ginger
1 t. salt

Combine all ingredients until smooth and evenly mixed.

Farmers' market foods taste so fresh because they're
all grown and picked in-season, at the peak of flavor...lettuce,
asparagus and strawberries in the springtime, tomatoes,
peppers and sweet corn in the summer, squash and
greens in the fall and winter.

Savory Winter Stew

Serves 5

1 T. oil
1 lb. Polish Kielbasa sausage,
  sliced
1 onion, sliced
8-oz. pkg. sliced mushrooms
1 yellow squash, cubed
1 clove garlic, minced

4 c. water
2 c. red cabbage, shredded
2 T. rice vinegar
1 T. brown sugar, packed
2 t. chicken bouillon granules
1/8 t. pepper

Heat oil in a saucepan over medium heat. Cook sausage, onion, mushrooms, squash and garlic in oil for 5 minutes, or until vegetables are tender. Add remaining ingredients. Bring to a boil; reduce heat to a simmer and cook for 15 to 20 minutes.

Over the weekend, prepare the week's salads ahead of time so tonight's dinner is quick & easy! Store salad in a slightly damp plastic zipping bag and refrigerate; it will be fresh for up to 4 days.

Cajun Skillet Rice

Serves 4

1 T. olive oil
1 c. onion, chopped
1 c. green pepper, chopped
1 c. red pepper, chopped
1 lb. Kielbasa sausage, sliced
2 t. Cajun seasoning

Optional: 1/8 t. cayenne pepper
14-1/2 oz. can fire-roasted or
    plain diced tomatoes
1-1/2 c. chicken broth
3/4 c. long-cooking rice,
    uncooked

Heat oil in a large skillet over medium-high heat. Add onion, peppers
and sausage; sprinkle with desired seasonings. Sauté until onion is
translucent, peppers have softened and sausage is lightly golden. Add
undrained tomatoes, broth and uncooked rice. Bring to a simmer; turn
heat to medium-low and cover. Cook for 20 minutes, or until all liquid
is absorbed and rice is tender.

To keep bacon slices from sticking together, roll the package into a tube shape and secure with a rubber band before storing in the refrigerator. Makes them so easy to use when you're ready!

Bacon, Rice & Tomatoes

Serves 4 to 6

1-lb. pkg. bacon, chopped and
    crisply cooked, drippings
    reserved
14-1/2 oz. can stewed tomatoes

1/4 c. water
1 T. sugar
salt and pepper to taste
3 c. cooked rice

Combine cooked bacon, tomatoes, water and sugar in a large skillet over medium heat; stir well. Add 1/4 cup reserved bacon drippings; reduce heat to medium-low. Cook for 15 minutes; add salt and pepper. Cook for an additional 5 minutes; serve over rice.

Cook egg noodles the easy way, no watching needed. Bring water
to a rolling boil, then turn off heat. Add noodles and let stand
for 20 minutes, stirring twice. Drain well and toss with
a little butter...ready to serve!

Asian-Style Pork & Noodles

Serves 4

3/4 c. orange juice
1/4 c. hoisin sauce
3 T. cider vinegar
2 T. catsup
3/4 t. salt
8-oz. pkg. wide egg noodles,
    uncooked
1 bunch broccoli, separated into
    flowerets, stalks thinly sliced

1/2 lb. sugar snap peas or
    snow peas, trimmed
2 T. oil
1 lb. boneless pork loin, cut into
    1/2-inch wide strips
3 T. cornstarch

In a small bowl, stir together orange juice, hoisin sauce, vinegar, catsup and salt; set aside. Cook noodles according to package directions, just until tender, adding broccoli and peas during last minute of cooking. Drain; transfer to a large bowl. Meanwhile, heat oil in a large skillet over medium heat. Dredge pork in cornstarch, shaking off excess. Sauté pork until lightly golden and no longer pink in the center, tossing frequently, about 3 minutes. Pour in orange juice mixture; stir and bring to a boil. Add pork to noodle mixture; toss to combine.

Garlicky orzo is a tasty side for any main dish. Sauté 2 cloves chopped garlic in 2 tablespoons butter until garlic is golden. Remove from heat and stir in one tablespoon lemon juice, one cup cooked orzo and 2 tablespoons chopped parsley.

Sausage Orzo Skillet

Makes 4 servings

1 lb. ground pork sausage
14-1/2 oz. can beef broth
14-1/2 oz. can stewed tomatoes

1-1/4 c. orzo pasta, uncooked
Optional: Italian seasoning
   to taste

In a skillet over medium heat, brown sausage; drain. Add broth and tomatoes with juice; bring to a boil. Stir in orzo; sprinkle with Italian seasoning, if using. Cover and simmer for 15 minutes, or until orzo is tender.

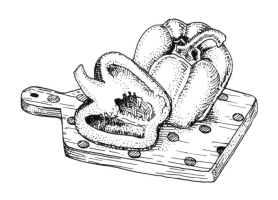

When freezing leftover sliced peppers, sweet onions, corn or
fresh herbs, add a little olive oil to the freezer bag and shake.
The oil will help keep pieces separate and fresher too. They'll be
ready to drop into sauces, salsas and salads!

Pepper & Onion Brats

Makes 6 servings

1 T. canola oil
2 onions, chopped
2 green peppers, thinly sliced
6 smoked bratwurst sausages

salt and pepper to taste
6 hot dog buns, split
Garnish: mustard

Heat oil in a large skillet over medium heat. Add onions, peppers and bratwursts. Cover and cook for about 5 minutes. Uncover; continue cooking until onions are translucent and golden. Add salt and pepper to taste. Place a brat and some of the onion mixture on each hot dog bun; top generously with mustard.

Which apple is best? The tastiest pie apples are
Rome, Jonathan, Fuji and Granny Smith. For salads,
try McIntosh, Red Delicious, Empire and Gala.

Ham Steak & Apples Skillet

Makes 6 servings

3 T. butter
1/2 c. brown sugar, packed
1 T. Dijon mustard

2 c. apples, cored and diced
2 1-lb. cooked bone-in ham
   steaks

Melt butter in a large skillet over medium heat. Add brown sugar and
mustard; bring to a simmer. Add apples; cover and simmer for 5 minutes.
Top apple mixture with ham steaks. Cover with a lid; simmer for about
10 minutes more, until apples are tender. Remove ham to a platter
and cut into serving-size pieces. Top ham with apples and sauce.

Freeze chicken breasts or pork chops with their marinades in airtight containers. By the time it's frozen and thawed for cooking, the meat will have absorbed just enough flavor... so easy and delicious!

Zesty Zippy Italian Chops

Makes 4 servings

4 boneless pork chops
1 T. oil
1-1/2 c. zesty Italian salad
    dressing

1 onion, finely chopped
salt and pepper to taste

Brown pork chops on both sides in oil in a skillet over medium-high heat, about 3 minutes. Stir in salad dressing and onion. Cover and cook over medium-low heat for about 25 minutes.

Create a cozy Italian restaurant feel for your get-together.
Toss a red & white checked tablecloth over the table, light drip
candles in empty bottles and add a basket of garlic bread.

Pepper Bacon-Tomato Linguine

Serves 6

16-oz. pkg. linguine pasta,
  uncooked
1/2 lb. peppered bacon, diced
2 T. green onions, chopped
2 t. garlic, minced

14-1/2 oz. can diced tomatoes
1 t. dried basil
salt and pepper to taste
3 T. grated Parmesan cheese

Cook pasta according to package directions; drain. Meanwhile, in a large
skillet over medium heat, cook bacon until crisp. Remove bacon to a
paper towel; reserve drippings in skillet. Add onion and garlic to
drippings; sauté for one minute. Stir in tomatoes with juice and
seasonings; simmer for 5 minutes. Add linguine, Parmesan cheese
and bacon; toss to mix well.

Beans add flavor and fiber to hearty recipes...
try mashed cannellini, kidney, black or pinto beans
in place of, or in addition to, ground beef.

Southern Sausage & Pintos

Serves 5 to 6

1 lb. pork sausage links
1 onion, chopped
1 green pepper, chopped

2 15-oz. cans pinto beans,
   drained
8-oz. can tomato sauce

Cook sausages until browned on all sides in a large skillet over
medium heat; drain all but 2 tablespoons drippings. Cut each sausage
into thirds; return to skillet. Add onion and green pepper; sauté until
tender. Add remaining ingredients. Stir and simmer for 10 minutes,
until heated through.

Out of bread crumbs for a casserole? Just substitute
crushed herb-flavored stuffing mix instead and
it will be just as tasty.

Patsy's Stuffed Pork Chops

Makes 8 servings

2 6-oz. pkgs. stuffing mix
8 boneless pork chops
2 T. oil
3 cloves garlic, sliced

salt and pepper to taste
2 c. applesauce
cinnamon to taste

Prepare stuffing mixes according to package instructions; set aside.
Slicing horizontally into the sides, cut a pocket into the center of each
pork chop. Evenly stuff chops with prepared stuffing. Drizzle oil and
sprinkle garlic in a 13"x9" baking pan. Arrange chops in pan and season
with salt and pepper. Top each chop with 1/4 cup applesauce and sprinkle
with cinnamon. Bake, uncovered, at 425 degrees for 30 minutes, or until
chops are no longer pink.

Only using half an onion? Rub the cut side with butter or olive oil,
store in the fridge in a plastic zipping bag, and it will
stay fresh for weeks.

Smoked Sausage & Veggies

Makes 4 servings

1 lb. smoked pork sausage,
    thinly sliced
4 potatoes, cooked and cubed
1 sweet onion, cut into chunks

1 green pepper, cut into chunks
Optional: cooked rice or egg
    noodles

In a skillet over medium heat, combine all ingredients except rice or
noodles. Cook until onion and pepper are tender and sausage is browned.
Serve over cooked rice or noodles, if desired.

Fast and fun! Whip up several different kinds of sandwiches
(or stop at the local deli for a few!) and cut each one into
4 sections. Arrange them all on a large platter with chips and
pickles...everyone will love the variety and it couldn't be easier.

Swiss Ham Buns

Makes 12 servings

1/4 c. mustard
1/4 c. mayonnaise-type salad
  dressing
2 T. onion, finely chopped
1/2 t. salt

1/8 t. pepper
12 hamburger buns, split
12 slices deli ham
12 slices baby Swiss cheese

Mix together mustard, salad dressing, onion, salt and pepper. Spread
mixture on cut sides of buns. Top each bun with one slice of ham and
one slice of cheese. Wrap buns individually in aluminum foil; place
on a baking sheet. Bake at 350 degrees for 25 minutes, or until
heated through.

After you unpack groceries, take just a little time to prep ingredients and place them in plastic zipping bags...wash and chop fruits and vegetables and separate into servings. Weeknight dinners will be so much easier.

Carol's Veggie Panini

Makes 4 servings

2 T. balsamic vinegar
1 T. olive oil
1/2 t. salt
1/8 t. pepper
1 eggplant, cut into 1/4-inch slices

1 zucchini, cut into 8 slices
1 red pepper, quartered
8 slices ciabatta bread
1 c. shredded mozzarella cheese
8 fresh basil leaves

Whisk vinegar, oil, salt and pepper in a bowl; set aside. Brush both sides of eggplant and zucchini with vinegar mixture. Arrange in a single layer on a lightly greased baking sheet. Coat vegetables with non-stick vegetable spray. Broil about 4 inches from heat for 7 to 8 minutes, turning once and coating vegetables with spray as needed. Lightly brush one side of each bread slice with remaining vinegar mixture; turn and coat second side with spray. Place bread, sprayed-side down, on an ungreased baking sheet. Top with vegetables, cheese and basil. Top with remaining bread slices, sprayed-side up. Place sandwiches, one at a time, in a skillet; set a bacon press or other weight on top. Cook sandwiches over medium-high heat for about 4 minutes, turning once, until lightly golden on both sides.

Zucchini and other summer squash make tasty side dishes and are easily swapped out in recipes. Try substituting old-fashioned yellow crookneck or pattypan squash for zucchini in any favorite recipe.

Golden Zucchini Patties

Makes 6 to 8

3-1/2 c. zucchini, grated
3 T. onion, grated
2 T. fresh parsley, minced
1/3 c. grated Parmesan cheese
1 c. soft bread crumbs

1 t. salt
1/2 t. pepper
2 eggs, beaten
3/4 c. dry bread crumbs
1/2 c. butter, melted

Wrap zucchini in paper towels; press out as much liquid as possible.
Combine zucchini, onion, parsley, cheese, soft bread crumbs, salt, pepper
and eggs. Shape into patties; dip into dry bread crumbs. Place on greased
baking sheets; drizzle with butter. Bake at 350 degrees for 30 to
40 minutes, until golden.

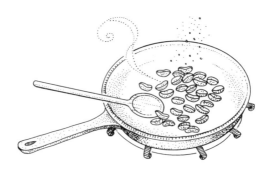

Sugared nuts are scrumptious tossed over a crisp garden salad. Add 3/4 cup pecans or walnuts, 1/4 cup sugar and one teaspoon butter to a cast-iron skillet. Cook and stir over medium heat for about 7 minutes, or until sugar is golden and melted. Spread carefully on a greased baking sheet and let cool completely.

Grilled Salmon Salad

Serves 2 to 4

10 to 12-oz. salmon fillet
1/2 c. lime juice
pepper to taste
4 c. spinach, torn
1 c. sweetened dried cranberries
1 c. crumbled blue cheese
1 c. sugared walnuts
1 tomato, sliced
vinaigrette or blue cheese salad
   dressing to taste

Dip both sides of salmon in lime juice; sprinkle with pepper. Grill over medium-high heat for 4 to 5 minutes per side, until fish flakes easily. Divide remaining ingredients except salad dressing between 2 plates. Slice salmon in half or quarters; place on plates. Drizzle with desired amount of salad dressing.

Minted peas are a fast and fresh side. Place a small package of frozen baby peas in a skillet over medium heat. Cook and stir until peas are just cooked through. Add one tablespoon butter, 1/2 teaspoon sugar, 2 teaspoons snipped fresh mint and a few drops of lemon juice. Toss until mixed well and serve hot.

Sea Green Linguine

Serves 4

16-oz. pkg. linguine or spaghetti
    pasta, uncooked
1/2 c. onion, diced
2 cloves garlic, minced
3 T. olive oil

2 6-oz. cans chopped clams,
    drained and liquid reserved
15-1/4 oz. can peas, drained
Garnish: grated Parmesan cheese

Cook pasta according to package directions; drain and set aside.
Meanwhile, in a saucepan, sauté onion and garlic in oil over low heat
until soft. Add reserved liquid from clams; bring to a simmer. Add clams;
warm through. Remove from heat. In a serving bowl, toss peas with
pasta; pour clam mixture over top. Sprinkle with Parmesan cheese.

Turn hot dog buns into garlic bread sticks in a jiffy!
Spread with softened butter, sprinkle with garlic salt and
broil until toasty. Thrifty and tasty!

Macaroni Cheese Twists

16-oz. pkg. rotini pasta,
    uncooked
1/2 c. green pepper, diced
1 clove garlic, minced
1 c. onion, chopped
1 T. olive oil
2 8-oz. cans tomato sauce

1 c. water
2 T. fresh parsley, chopped
1/2 t. dried oregano
1/4 lb. pasteurized process cheese
    spread, cubed
Optional: grated Parmesan cheese

Cook pasta according to package directions; drain. Meanwhile, in a
saucepan over medium heat, sauté green pepper, garlic and onion in
olive oil until tender. Stir in tomato sauce, water and herbs. Reduce heat;
simmer for 10 minutes. Transfer pasta to a large serving bowl; add
cheese cubes and toss until melted. Spoon tomato sauce mixture over
pasta mixture; toss well. Serve immediately, sprinkled with Parmesan
cheese, if desired.

Take the children to a pick-your-own farm or
local farmers' market. Later they'll be much more willing
to eat "their" fruits & vegetables.

Easy Fettuccine Primavera

Serves 6

12-oz. pkg. fettuccine pasta,
    uncooked
1/2 c. creamy Italian salad
    dressing
1 c. broccoli flowerets
1 c. zucchini, sliced
1 c. red pepper, thinly sliced

1/2 c. onion, chopped
1/2 t. dried basil
1/2 c. butter
2 tomatoes, chopped
1/2 c. sliced mushrooms
Garnish: grated Parmesan cheese

Cook pasta according to package directions; drain. Toss warm pasta with
salad dressing; stir to coat. Set aside; cover to keep warm. Meanwhile,
in a skillet over medium heat, cook broccoli, zucchini, pepper, onion and
basil in butter until tender. Stir in tomatoes and mushrooms; cook just
until heated through. Toss vegetable mixture with warm pasta mixture.
Garnish with Parmesan cheese.

Eggplants stay fresh just a few days, so it's best to keep them stored in the crisper of the refrigerator, unwrapped. This way, they'll be ready for any garden-fresh recipe for one week.

Stuffed Eggplant Boats

Serves 4

2 eggplants, peeled and halved
    lengthwise
1 t. salt
2 potatoes, peeled and chopped
4 T. olive oil, divided
1 c. onion, diced

1 red pepper, diced
2 cloves garlic, minced
salt and pepper to taste
8-oz. pkg. shredded mozzarella
    cheese
1 c. dry bread crumbs

Scoop out the centers of eggplants to form boats. Lightly salt boats; spray with non-stick vegetable spray on all sides. Set aside on a greased baking sheet. In a skillet, cook potatoes in 3 tablespoons olive oil until golden. Remove with a slotted spoon to a separate plate. Add onion, red pepper and garlic to skillet. Cook until onion is translucent and pepper is tender. Return potatoes to pan; sprinkle with salt and pepper to taste. Fill eggplant boats with mixture. Top with cheese and bread crumbs; drizzle with remaining oil. Bake at 350 degrees for 30 minutes, or until tender. Serve immediately.

Mix up the ingredients for a quick & easy side-salad in a plastic zipping bag, and it'll be done in half the time. Just blend by shaking and spoon out individual servings.

Tortellini Blue Cheese Alfredo

Serves 4 to 6

20-oz. pkg. refrigerated tortellini
    pasta, uncooked
2 T. butter
4 to 5 shallots, minced
1 T. all-purpose flour

1-2/3 c. half-and-half
4-oz. container crumbled blue
    cheese
Optional: white pepper to taste

Cook pasta according to package directions; drain and set aside. In a
skillet over medium heat, melt butter. Sauté shallots in butter until soft;
do not brown. Add flour and mix well. Slowly add half-and-half while
stirring constantly. Cook, stirring occasionally, until sauce thickens,
about 5 to 8 minutes. After sauce thickens, add blue cheese and allow
to melt into sauce. Add pepper, if desired. Toss pasta with sauce; serve
immediately.

Fresh mozzarella is delicious on casserole dishes but can be difficult to grate. Freeze it first! Wrap a block of mozzarella in plastic wrap and freeze for 20 minutes; then grate. Store the grated cheese in a resealable plastic zipping bag in the refrigerator for up to 5 days.

Easy Cheesy Ratatouille

Serves 6 to 8

1 eggplant, peeled and cut into 1-inch cubes
1 onion, diced
1 red pepper, diced
1 zucchini, cut into 1-inch cubes
1/4 c. sun-dried tomato vinaigrette
14-1/2 oz. can diced tomatoes
1/4 c. grated Parmesan cheese
1 c. shredded mozzarella cheese

Sauté vegetables with vinaigrette in a large oven-safe skillet over medium heat. Add tomatoes with juice; cook for 15 minutes. Sprinkle with cheeses. Bake, uncovered, at 350 degrees for 15 minutes, or until vegetables are tender.

Stir up a dilly of a sauce for salmon patties. Whisk together
1/2 cup sour cream, one tablespoon Dijon mustard,
one tablespoon lemon juice and 2 teaspoons chopped
fresh dill. Chill...so simple and so good!

Salmon Cornbread Cakes

Serves 6

2 T. mayonnaise
2 eggs, beaten
1 t. dried parsley
3 green onions, thinly sliced
1 t. seafood seasoning

1 to 2 t. Worcestershire sauce
14-3/4 oz. can salmon, drained
    and bones removed
2 c. cornbread, crumbled
1 T. canola oil

In a bowl, combine mayonnaise, eggs, parsley, green onions, seafood seasoning and Worcestershire sauce. Stir well. Mix in salmon and cornbread. Shape into 6 to 8 patties. Heat oil in a skillet over medium heat. Cook patties in oil for 3 to 4 minutes on each side, until golden.

Oops! If a soup or stew begins to burn on the bottom,
all is not lost. Spoon it into another pan, being careful
not to scrape up the scorched food on the bottom.
The burnt taste usually won't linger.

Buttery Cabbage & Noodles

Makes 8 to 10 servings

1 yellow onion, chopped
1/4 c. plus 1 to 2 T. butter,
    divided
1 head cabbage, chopped

16-oz. pkg. wide egg noodles or
    bowtie pasta, uncooked
garlic powder, salt and pepper
    to taste

In a stockpot over medium heat, sauté onion in 1/4 cup butter until translucent. Add cabbage; stir until onion and cabbage are well mixed. Cover; simmer over low heat for 45 minutes to an hour, stirring occasionally. Cabbage will cook down. Meanwhile, cook noodles or pasta according to package directions; drain. When cabbage is done cooking, add seasonings to taste. Fold noodles or pasta into cabbage mixture; stir in remaining butter. Cook over low heat until butter is melted.

Set a leaf placecard at each dinner guest's place.
Write each name on a leaf using a gold or silver pen...
try bright green leaves in summer, beautiful red or
orange fallen leaves in autumn.

Fishermen's Stew

Makes 6 to 8 servings

2 t. olive oil
2 c. turkey Kielbasa sausage,
    diced
2 onions, chopped
4 c. chicken broth
8-oz. bottle clam juice
2 6-oz. cans chopped clams
3/4 to 1 lb. cod or halibut,
    cut into 1-inch cubes

15-oz. can chickpeas, drained
    and rinsed
1 sweet potato, peeled and cubed
1 bay leaf
2 t. lemon juice
1/4 t. pepper

Heat oil in a large saucepan. Add Kielbasa and onions; stir until onions soften. Stir in broth, clam juice, clams with juice, fish, chickpeas, sweet potato and bay leaf. Simmer until fish is opaque and sweet potato is tender, about 10 minutes. Before serving, discard bay leaf; stir in lemon juice and pepper.

Turn an old wagon wheel into a mini herb garden right outside your kitchen door. Plant basil, thyme, chives, oregano and other fragrant herbs between the spokes...ready for snipping!

Bruschetta Pizza

Serves 6

10 roma tomatoes, chopped
5 to 6 cloves garlic, minced
2 T. fresh basil, chopped
1/2 red onion, finely chopped
1/4 c. plus 1 T. olive oil, divided
1/2 t. pepper
1/4 t. garlic salt

1/4 c. balsamic vinegar
13.8-oz. tube refrigerated pizza
   crust dough
1/2 c. pizza sauce
8-oz. pkg. shredded Italian-blend
   cheese
dried oregano to taste

In a large bowl, combine tomatoes, garlic, basil, onion, 1/4 cup oil, pepper, garlic salt and vinegar. Stir to blend; drain. Place pizza crust dough on an ungreased baking sheet. Spread with pizza sauce. Top with 1-1/2 to 2 cups tomato mixture. Sprinkle on cheese and oregano. Drizzle remaining oil over top. Bake according to pizza crust dough package directions.

Serve up homemade lemonade for a refreshing change...
it couldn't be simpler! In a large saucepan, combine 2 quarts
water and 1/2 cup sugar. Heat just until the sugar dissolves.
Remove from heat and pour in 3/4 cup lemon juice.
Mix well and chill.

Lemon Herb & Garlic Shrimp

Makes 4 to 6 servings

2 cloves garlic, pressed
2 T. olive oil
6 T. butter, sliced

1 lb. frozen cooked shrimp
1.8-oz. pkg. lemon herb soup mix
1 c. warm water

In a skillet over medium heat, sauté garlic in olive oil and butter for
2 minutes. Add shrimp and simmer until shrimp thaws, stirring often.
Dissolve soup mix in water; pour over shrimp mixture. Reduce heat;
simmer until heated through, about 20 minutes.

Turn up the heat! Try using extra-spicy salsa, Mexican-blend cheese or hot ground pork sausage in a familiar (but bland) recipe for extra zing!

Seafood Enchiladas

3 c. chicken broth
1/3 c. all-purpose flour
14-1/2 oz. can diced tomatoes
3 green chiles, chopped
1/2 c. onion, chopped
1/2 t. garlic, minced
1 t. sugar
1 t. ground cumin
1/2 t. dried basil

1/2 t. dried oregano
salt and pepper to taste
1 lb. crabmeat, flaked
1/2 lb. cooked shrimp
12-oz. pkg. shredded Monterey
  Jack cheese
12 10-inch flour tortillas
3/4 c. sour cream

Combine broth with flour in a saucepan. Cook over medium heat until thickened, stirring constantly. Add tomatoes with juice, chiles, onion, garlic, sugar and seasonings. Bring to a simmer, stirring frequently. Remove from heat. Divide seafood and half of cheese evenly among tortillas; roll up and arrange seam-side down in a greased 15"x10" jelly-roll pan. Blend sour cream into tomato mixture. Spoon tomato mixture over enchiladas; sprinkle with remaining cheese. Bake, uncovered, at 400 degrees for 15 minutes, or until cheese melts.

INDEX

INDEX

Our Story

Back in 1984, we were next-door neighbors raising our families in the little town of Delaware, Ohio. Two moms with small children, we were looking for a way to do what we loved and stay home with the kids too. We had always shared a love of home cooking and making memories with family & friends and so, after many a conversation over the backyard fence, **Gooseberry Patch** was born.

We put together our first catalog at our kitchen tables, enlisting the help of our loved ones wherever we could. From that very first mailing, we found an immediate connection with many of our customers and it wasn't long before we began receiving letters, photos and recipes from these new friends. In 1992, we put together our very first cookbook, compiled from hundreds of these recipes and, the rest, as they say, is history.

Hard to believe it's been over 25 years since those kitchen-table days! From that original little **Gooseberry Patch** family, we've grown to include an amazing group of creative folks who love cooking, decorating and creating as much as we do. Today, we're best known for our homestyle, family-friendly cookbooks, now recognized as national bestsellers.

One thing's for sure, we couldn't have done it without our friends all across the country. Each year, we're honored to turn thousands of your recipes into our collectible cookbooks. Our hope is that each book captures the stories and heart of all of you who have shared with us. Whether you've been with us since the beginning or are just discovering us, welcome to the **Gooseberry Patch** family!

JoAnn & Vickie

Visit our website anytime
www.gooseberrypatch.com

Email Club

Blog

You Tube

1•800•854•6673